BESSIE COLEMAN

Philip S. Hart

In Consultation with Martha Cosgrove,
M.A. and Reading Specialist

Lerner Publications Company / Minneapolis

Martha Cosgrove has a master's degree from the University of Minnesota in secondary education, with an emphasis on developmental and remedial reading. She is licensed in 7–12 English and language arts, developmental reading, and remedial reading. She has had several works published, and she gives numerous state and national presentations in her areas of expertise.

Lerner Publications Company
A division of Lerner Publishing Group
241 First Avenue North
Minneapolis, Minnesota U.S.A.

Website address: www.lernerbooks.com

Library of Congress Cataloging-in-Publication Data

Hart, Philip S.
    Bessie Coleman / by Philip S. Hart.
       p.   cm. – (Just the facts biographies)
    Includes bibliographical references and index.
    ISBN: 0–8225–2469–4 (lib. bdg. : alk. paper)
    1. Coleman, Bessie, 1896–1926–Juvenile literature. 2. African American women air pilots–Biography–Juvenile literature. 3. Air pilots–United States–Biography–Juvenile literature. I. Title. II. Series.
    TL540.C546H37 2005
    629.13'092–dc22   2004027918

Manufactured in the United States of America
1 2 3 4 5 6 – JR – 10 09 08 07 06 05

Contents

1

DREAMING OF FLYING

IN 1910, EIGHTEEN-YEAR-OLD Bessie Coleman was up late again, doing schoolwork. She was preparing for her writing course. Bessie's writing teacher had the students read newspaper articles. The students were then asked to rewrite them in their own words. One article Bessie was rewriting was about the famous American flyers Wilbur and Orville Wright. They had built an airplane with an engine. Then they had made the world's first engine-powered flight at Kitty Hawk, North Carolina, in 1903.

In the early 1900s, flying was a new and exciting adventure. Bessie and other students in her

The first powered airplane flight was made by Orville Wright at Kitty Hawk, North Carolina, in 1903. It lasted twelve seconds.

writing class were wide eyed when they read about the daring Wright brothers. They also learned about Raymonde de Laroche, a Frenchwoman who had recently become the first female to earn a pilot's license. Bessie had been surprised to learn that women flew planes. But the reaction of some of her friends and classmates surprised her even more.

Many people in the early 1900s thought that women had no business sitting behind the controls of an airplane. Flying was dangerous, they said, and women belonged at home. But such talk didn't impress Bessie much. She knew that women were capable of all kinds of things. At least, *she* meant to do something unusual with her life.

EARLY DAYS

Bessie Coleman was born to George and Susan Coleman on January 26, 1892. She and her many brothers and sisters first lived in Atlanta, Texas. The family moved to the mostly African American section of Waxahachie, Texas, two years later. Eventually, the

Bessie and her family lived in this house in Waxahachie, Texas.

Coleman family grew to include three sisters younger than Bessie.

George Coleman was part African American and part Native American. His grandparents had lived on an Indian reservation in what was then called Indian Territory. This area

IT'S A FACT!
George and Susan Coleman had thirteen children. Only nine of them, including Bessie, lived past their childhood years.

would later become part of the state of Oklahoma.

When Bessie was growing up, American society was strictly segregated, or separated. African American children and white children didn't go to school together. The two groups didn't live in the same neighborhoods, and African Americans didn't have the same chances for jobs. Life was hard for African American families like Bessie's. George Coleman had difficulty finding work to support his large family. He grew very frustrated with his situation.

Meanwhile, Bessie grew up and started school in a small, crowded classroom at Waxahachie's African American school. She loved learning and was a hardworking student. She was eager to learn new things. She was particularly good at math and could add and subtract in her head faster than most of the other students. By the time she was nine, Bessie Coleman stood out as the small, pretty student who did well in nearly all subjects.

But things were about to change. Bessie's father still couldn't find ongoing work. In 1901, he left his family in Texas and went to Indian Territory. As a Native American, he had better chances in Indian Territory than he had in Texas. He hoped to find better job opportunities. But he couldn't convince Susan and his children to go with him. He left Texas with a heavy heart.

IT'S A FACT!

The U.S. government first organized the land called Indian Territory in the 1820s. It was joined with the Oklahoma Territory in 1906, becoming the state of Oklahoma in 1907.

After George left, Susan Coleman had to support the family. She found work as a maid in white households around Waxahachie. By this time, the older Coleman children had already moved away from home. Walter and John, two of Bessie's older brothers, were living far to the north, in the large city of Chicago, Illinois. This left nine-year-old Bessie as the oldest child still at home. She stopped going to school to look after her three younger sisters—Elois, Nilus, and baby Georgia—while her mother worked.

Downtown Chicago was filled with streetcars, buggies, and people on foot in the early 1900s.

IN CHARGE

Bessie was in charge of the Coleman household in Waxahachie. Her chores included keeping the house neat and clean. She watched over her sisters as they played in the yard by her mother's rosebushes. She cooked their lunches on the woodstove. Bessie made sure they'd washed behind their ears. Sometimes, she took them out back to wade in Mustang Creek.

Bessie didn't really mind all the work, and she loved her little sisters. But she still remembered when things had been different. She used to play in the front yard too. And she used to go to school every day. She missed going to school terribly. But until little Georgia could make the four-mile walk to school with her, Bessie would be going there only now and again.

Another job that Bessie had was to pick cotton during harvesttime. Late each summer, when the white tufts of cotton were ready for picking, African American families all around Waxahachie gathered to work in the fields. So many children helped out that the school Bessie had gone to closed until after the harvest was done. Families were paid a certain amount for each sack filled with cotton.

Throughout the South, when cotton was ready for picking, entire families harvested the crop.

Working in the cotton fields convinced Bessie she didn't want to spend the rest of her life picking cotton. It was hot and humid in the fields, and the workdays were very long. The sacks filled with cotton were heavy and hard for someone as small as Bessie to carry or drag.

Even though Bessie didn't much like working in the fields, she knew the family needed her to earn money. Her strong math skills also came in very handy. Bessie could add up what her family was owed so fast that none of the landowners around Waxahachie would dare underpay the Colemans.

AT SCHOOL AGAIN

One way to be sure of staying out of the cotton fields was to get more education. When her sisters were older, Bessie went back to school. All that time away from school hadn't made her any less interested in learning. She finished eighth grade at the Waxahachie school. Bessie wanted even more education. But this would cost money. She started doing laundry for white people as a way to make money. Susan Coleman encouraged her daughter.

By 1910, Bessie had saved enough money to move to Oklahoma. She enrolled in Langston College in Langston, Oklahoma. This college for African Americans was based on the idea that hard work would lead to progress in America. Part of Langston was set up for students who had not yet received enough education to go to the full college. The idea was that these students would take classes that would prepare them for the challenge of the full college.

Bessie was a hard worker. She had completed school with better than average grades, even though she'd been caring for her younger sisters and picking cotton. Bessie didn't know exactly what she wanted to do after she got more schooling. But she knew she wanted a better life than the one she'd lived in Texas.

LANGSTON COLLEGE

In the 1890s, African American settlers in Langston, Indian Territory, began raising money to start the Colored Agricultural and Normal University. In 1898, they had enough money to purchase forty acres of land to start the school, which later came to be called Langston College. Dr. Inman E. Page, the son of a former slave, became the school's first president.

Langston's goal was to educate African American men and women so they could excel in jobs in farming, mechanics, and industry. The first bachelor's degree was awarded in 1901. The school expanded, adding more classrooms and teachers over the years. The college changed its name to Langston University in 1941 and added many more areas of study, including a degree in airway science. The Federal Aviation Administration (FAA), the U.S. government agency that oversees everything to do with flying and planes, has approved this area of study.

Knowing her life would be better once she had more education didn't stop Bessie from being homesick. Langston was about 400 miles from Waxahachie. Sleeping in a strange bed meant Bessie barely slept at all. She missed her mother and sisters.

The teacher in one of her classes told Bessie that a white American woman had earned a pilot's license. Her name was Harriet Quimby. Bessie longed to find out more about Quimby and her flights, but studying was more important.

This is Page Hall—named after Dr. Inman Page—at Langston University in Oklahoma. The school was originally called the Colored Agricultural and Normal University.

Bessie's classes were going well during her first term at Langston. She wrote to her mother and sisters in Waxahachie regularly. They were proud of Bessie, but things at home were not going smoothly with Bessie gone. As the year went on, Susan Coleman was able to send less and less money to her daughter. Bessie was barely able to pay for her books.

Bessie wondered if she'd be able to remain in school much longer. She found it hard to concentrate on her schoolwork when her mother and sisters were struggling. As a result, Bessie's grades went down because of the money pressure. The cotton harvest at home had been bad. No more money was available for Bessie's schooling. In 1911, she was forced to quit school. With her spirits down, Bessie headed back home.

2 MOVING TO CHICAGO

AT ABOUT THIS TIME, it's likely that Bessie
wrote to her older brother Walter in Chicago. For
several years, Walter had been living in Chicago
with his wife, Willie. Bessie told Walter of having to
quit school and of not wanting to go back home.
She wondered if she could come to Chicago and
live with him. Bessie didn't receive a quick answer
from her brother.

WORKING HARD, GOING NOWHERE

Still waiting to hear from Walter, Bessie arrived
back in Waxahachie with mixed feelings. Bessie told
her mother she wanted to go to Chicago. Susan

Coleman wasn't too sure of the plan. She insisted Bessie was needed at home.

Looking at how hard her mother worked to keep the family together, Bessie couldn't argue. She settled back into life in Waxahachie, but she wasn't happy about it. She worked as a maid for white families, saving as much money as she could. After long days cleaning, doing laundry, and cooking, Bessie would arrive home worn out. She missed college and longed to do something more with her life than washing and cooking and cleaning. To keep up her spirits, she figured out how much a one-way train ticket to Chicago would cost. She didn't tell her mother. She did tell her sister Georgia but swore her to secrecy.

One day, Bessie found a surprise when she returned home after a hard day. Sitting on her pillow in her bedroom was a letter from Walter. Bessie was so excited she tore apart the envelope. Walter encouraged Bessie to come to the city. He could give her a place to stay for a while. He also thought he could help her find work. Bessie ran to tell Georgia, but she was afraid to tell her mother. She decided to keep her secret until the time was right.

TAKING ACTION

That time wasn't too long in coming. In 1912, while dusting the house of the family she worked for, Bessie noticed a front-page newspaper article. The article told of Harriet Quimby's death in a plane crash in Massachusetts. Surprised and shocked, Bessie sat down heavily in a chair. She had not really thought of Harriet Quimby since leaving school.

Harriet Quimby was the first American woman to be licensed as a pilot.

HARRIET QUIMBY

Bessie was not alone in admiring Harriet Quimby, the first U.S. woman to earn a pilot's license. Harriet had become well known through her articles in *Leslie's Illustrated Weekly,* a popular national newspaper. She wrote about things that mattered to working women of the day—such as how to budget money, how to find a job, and how to find a safe place to live.

In 1906, as part of her job as a writer for *Leslie's,* Harriet went to the Belmont Park International Aviation Tournament in New York. She fell in love with flying while at the tournament. She met the Moisant family, who operated a flying school. Alfred Moisant agreed to teach Harriet to fly. The story of her lessons became an ongoing feature of *Leslie's,* until Harriet earned her pilot's license in August 1911.

Harriet then went on to make a name for herself in aviation. She was the first woman to make a nighttime flight. She was the first woman to cross the English Channel, flying from Dover in England to Hardelot in France. She then took up flying in exhibition air shows. She was killed after being thrown from her plane in an accident during an exhibition in 1912.

Bessie had just turned twenty. In an unexplained way, Harriet Quimby's death shook Bessie into action.

With Walter's letter in hand, Bessie approached her mother. Trying to speak with a stern, sure voice, Bessie told her mother that she wanted to head northward. Susan Coleman looked at her strong-willed daughter. Mrs. Coleman was well into her fifties, and her dreams had passed. With a heavy heart, she nodded her approval. One more child would be leaving home, heading north. She knew she couldn't hold back Bessie any longer.

Bessie wanted to leave for Chicago as soon as possible. But she was smart enough to know she needed to save more money. She worked for another three years. Those three years seemed like forever to Bessie.

This is the earliest-known photograph of Bessie. It shows her in 1920, in her her early twenties.

Finally, in 1915, she'd saved enough for the train trip north. She'd also made enough to leave some money with her mother and sisters. Her first-ever train journey on board the Rock Island Line to Chicago wasn't as exciting as Bessie thought it would be. She had to sit on a hard bench in the all-black section of the train. It was cramped and not nearly as comfortable as the

In the early 1900s, many African Americans moved north. In Chicago, some lived in neighborhoods like this one on the city's South Side.

rest of the train, which was set aside for white passengers.

The ride to Chicago took a full day. Bessie arrived at the South Side train station. She made her way to Walter's apartment on Forest Avenue. Walter and his wife, Willie, welcomed Bessie with open arms. Also on hand was her other brother, John, and his wife, Elizabeth.

WORK AND FUN

Walter told Bessie he thought he could get her a job as a maid with a white family on the north side of town. Bessie was grateful for Walter's help, but she didn't like this suggestion. She hadn't come all the way to Chicago to clean houses for white people just as she had done in Waxahachie. Walter then told her to check with local barbershops. Bessie was young and attractive. Walter thought there might be a place for his sister in the grooming business.

Following Walter's suggestion, Bessie learned how to manicure (care for) nails. Soon she landed a job as a manicurist at the White Sox Barber Shop on Chicago's South Side. Bessie became quite popular in her new job. She was a favorite

Pekin Café was located in the area along Chicago's State Street called the Stroll, where Bessie spent much of her free time.

manicurist of the shop's many young–and not so young–African American customers.

In the early 1900s, the South Side of Chicago was the center of the African American community. Bessie worked and spent most of her free time in an area called the Stroll. It stretched along State Street for nine blocks from Thirty-first to Thirty-ninth streets. The Stroll had shopping and entertainment. Dance clubs were everywhere. Bessie was able to dance to the music of great African

American performers, such as Louis Armstrong and Ethel Waters. But Bessie also came to learn that a bigger world existed beyond Chicago's South Side. This bigger part of Chicago was closed off to her because she was African American.

Still, to Bessie, Chicago was an exciting place. Certainly, it was much more exciting than

Louis Armstrong started his career as a jazz musician in Chicago in the 1920s.

IT'S A FACT!

Walter Coleman loved his little sister, but he couldn't understand her. He had introduced her to the best men on the South Side. Walter thought any young woman would jump at the chance to marry one of these fine young men. But Bessie had a mind of her own.

the small-town life she had left behind. Better yet, she was able to save money and send a bit back home to Waxahachie each month. Her letters to Georgia and the others were full of encouraging words.

In addition to earning her own way, Bessie was meeting young men in the shop and through Walter. She dated a few of them, but mostly she kept her distance. Bessie began to suspect that Walter wanted her to marry so she would move out. She knew she wasn't ready for marriage quite yet. Bessie had her dreams, and she didn't think marriage would help her achieve them.

GOING FOR HER DREAMS

Bessie had an active life. She was working hard at the shop, and she was meeting successful young men. She enjoyed spending time with her family. Yet, Bessie sometimes found herself reading and daydreaming. The Chicago papers carried many stories about one of Bessie's favorite topics—flying.

Two young white women, Ruth Law and Katherine Stinson, were making headlines flying in Chicago. Sometimes Bessie thought she heard the sound of an airplane engine buzzing overhead.

Pilot Ruth Law set a record with a nonstop flight from Chicago to Hornell, New York, in 1916.

She wondered what it would feel like to fly. Bessie didn't know what to make of her thoughts. But they were quite different from the busy hum of her work and everyday life.

Everyday life had its exciting moments too, however. By 1918, Bessie's mother and her sisters, Georgia, Elois, and Nilus and their children, had moved to Chicago. Bessie had been urging them to move northward for some time. She was glad they had finally joined her, Walter, and John.

At about the same time, Bessie married an older gentleman named Claude Glenn. Walter probably introduced Bessie and Claude. But the marriage still came as a surprise to the other Colemans. Bessie moved from Walter's house. But Bessie and Claude never seem to have lived under the same roof. Her family tried to figure out this relationship, but they knew Bessie was very independent. Over time, Claude seemed to simply disappear from Bessie's life.

INSPIRED BY BULLARD

Bessie was adjusting to many changes in her life in Chicago. For example, both of her brothers and many of her male friends on the South Side were being sent overseas. World War I (1914–1918) had been raging in Europe since 1914. By 1917, the United States was drawn into the war.

At that time, black and white soldiers served in separate units in the U.S. military. Rules barred African American soldiers from many military jobs, including becoming a pilot. These rules are forms of racial discrimination.

Because of this racial discrimination, a young African American named Eugene Bullard chose to serve with the French air service during World War I. Bullard couldn't find a flying teacher in the United States. He went to France because he had heard that, unlike the

IT'S A FACT!

Bessie's brothers were part of the Eighth Army National Guard, a part of the 370th Infantry. This segregated unit of the U.S. Army earned 121 American Distinguished Service Crosses and 68 French Croix de Guerre. Another all-African American army unit, the 369th American Expeditionary Force, would later be part of one of Bessie's exhibitions, or exciting air shows.

Eugene Bullard, an American citizen, flew for the French military during World War I.

United States, France had no problem giving African Americans a chance to excel in new jobs.

The *Chicago Defender,* a leading black weekly newspaper, wrote about Bullard's flying adventures in France. Along with other

Chicagoans, Bessie read about Bullard. She had
never heard of any African American person
flying a plane.

THE BLACK SWALLOW

Eugene Jacques Bullard was the world's first African American combat
pilot. He earned the nickname, the "Black Swallow of Death," in the early
1900s, while in the French Foreign Legion, a volunteer military unit.

Born in Georgia in 1894, Bullard and his family left the South after
members of the racist Ku Klux Klan organization terrorized his family. His
father had told him that in France, he'd be judged by his actions, not his
skin color. By his late teens, Bullard had stowed aboard a ship going to
Europe. By 1914, the year that World War 1 started between France and
Germany, he'd joined the French Foreign Legion. Between 1914 and
1916, he took part in some of the toughest land battles of the war.

While getting better after being wounded in battle, Bullard asked to be
able to join the French Flying Corps. In May 1917, he became the world's
first African American pilot. He flew twenty missions against German
forces, shooting down at least five German planes. He received French
awards for his bravery.

After the war, Bullard stayed in France. He supported himself by working
as an entertainer and eventually owned several music clubs. In the early
days of World War II (1939–1945)—when France was again at war
against Germany—Bullard was an important member of the French
Resistance. This group of people secretly fought against Germany, which
was fighting to occupy France. Resistance members were spies and
destroyed German equipment and supplies. In 1940, to avoid being
captured by the Germans, he went back to the United States. He lived in
Harlem, New York, until his death in 1961.

Bessie would search through the *Defender* each week to see if another story had appeared on Bullard's daring flights. She was proud to read that Eugene Bullard was awarded the Croix de Guerre, or Cross of War. This is the highest honor the French military can give. They gave it to Bullard for his achievements flying in combat. Bullard inspired Bessie to dream again of flying.

Movie newsreels—short films that a movie theater played before it started the longer main film—carried even more information about pilots

Bessie saw films of World War I combat airplanes like these at the movie theater.

and the war. When Bessie went to the movies, she was more eager to see the newsreel than she was to see the movie. She would look carefully at the newsreel to find Bullard's black face among the many white pilots. Like everything else in American society at that time, movie theaters were segregated. Whites and blacks went to separate theaters. Bessie went to movies at all-black theaters. The vision of the brave young African American pilot Eugene Bullard stayed with her.

DREAMS OF FLYING

Throughout the war, Bessie followed Bullard's story on film, on radio, and in the pages of the *Defender*. One day in the shop, she found herself manicuring the fingernails of the *Defender* editor and publisher, Robert S. Abbott. Abbott was in his mid-forties. He had founded the *Defender* in 1905. He was an educated, well-dressed, and important member of Chicago's African American community. Bessie listened carefully to the stories Abbott told about Chicago and about major members of the South Side community.

On a later day after the war had ended, Abbott was again in the shop waiting for his appointment with Bessie. Her brother John, who had served in the war in France, walked in. All the customers and Bessie turned to listen to John. He talked about the Frenchwomen he had seen and met during wartime. According to John, Frenchwomen talked differently, dressed differently, and walked differently than American women. Some, he claimed, even flew airplanes.

Bessie knew John was only trying to entertain the folks at the barbershop. But his words hit her like a brick. Even though she thought her brother was stretching the truth, she meant to give flying a try for herself if she could. Listening to John talk about Frenchwomen and their planes, Bessie made a decision. She simply had to find someone to teach her to fly like a bird.

Perhaps if Bessie had known how difficult her search would be, she wouldn't have started. The only African American pilot she knew about was Eugene Bullard, and he was still far away in France. During the next few months, Bessie talked to a number of pilots, all of them white, in and around Chicago. They weren't encouraging. They all told her that being an African American and a woman were against her. They believed she should

In 1909, Raymonde Laroche became the first woman in the world to have a pilot's license. She was from France.

be happy staying at home and on the ground. Their words rang in Bessie's ears over and over, but she wasn't discouraged. She thought she had a barbershop customer who just might be interested in helping her out.

BESSIE AND ROBERT ABBOTT

When Bessie Coleman visited Robert Abbott at the *Defender* offices, the busy publisher was willing to make time to hear her story. She had come to seek his advice about learning to fly. Abbott must have been impressed by Coleman's seriousness. He heard her out and then gave her idea some thought. Abbott knew the exciting news of an African American woman pilot could boost readership of the *Defender*. He also knew it would be difficult to find her a teacher.

Eugene Bullard had faced a lot of obstacles as an African American pilot. Bessie Coleman would face even greater obstacles because of being an African American and a woman. In the early 1900s, most people—black or white, male or female—didn't believe a woman could or should fly a plane. Abbott told Coleman he needed more time to think about what she had suggested. Then he set an appointment to meet with her at the shop the next week. They would discuss his research while she manicured his nails.

Bessie was a nervous wreck during the next few days. Time had never moved so slowly. Finally, Robert Abbott strolled in for his weekly manicure.

ROBERT SENGSTACKE ABBOTT

Born in Georgia in 1870, Robert Abbott beat the odds and became a highly educated African American scholar. He earned degrees from Claflin University and the Hampton Institute and a law degree from Kent Law School in Chicago.

His stepfather, John Sengstacke, published a local newspaper in Georgia, and Abbott had worked at a newspaper to help pay his school fees. Racial discrimination stopped Abbott from opening a law office in Chicago. He then turned his attention to printing, with the idea of starting a newspaper that he hoped would inspire African Americans.

The first issue of the *Chicago Defender* came out in 1905. Abbott did all the selling and writing. By 1912, the paper was selling on newsstands, and Abbott had the help of editors. They pushed the paper to cover sports, theater, and African American society.

By 1929, the *Defender* was selling 250,000 copies nationwide. It covered issues of racial conflict and racial equality and encouraged southern African Americans to move north. The paper became a voice for African American arts, business, and politics. Abbott died in 1940, but he had groomed his nephew John Sengstacke to take over the paper. The *Defender* is still being published.

Sitting face-to-face, Coleman buffed Abbott's nails and glanced quickly at his eyes. Abbott told Bessie she should go to France. His research confirmed that it would be nearly impossible to find a teacher for her either in the United States or in Canada.

Robert S. Abbott was the editor and publisher of the *Defender* **and a supporter of Bessie's dream of flying.**

The French were much more accepting of women and of African Americans. And the French loved flying. Abbott also said Bessie's goal wasn't going to be easy to reach. She'd first have to learn to speak French. Bessie was so excited, she had trouble settling down. But she started learning French and was soon thinking, eating, and dreaming in the French language.

3 FLYING IN EUROPE

FOR THE NEXT FEW MONTHS,
whenever Bessie saw Robert Abbott, she'd
speak to him in French. Abbott would laugh
and praise her efforts to learn a new language.
Weeks passed, and Bessie became more and
more comfortable with her French lessons. She
also read about French culture. As her
language skills improved and her confidence

(Above)
**A plane flies
over the
European
countryside
in the 1920s.**

increased, Bessie decided to set a firm deadline for her trip. She'd been saving money for a long time. She found out the price of a train ticket to New York City. Then she learned the cost of a ticket on a steamship that would travel across the Atlantic Ocean to Europe.

DECIDING TO FLY

By this time, she had told Walter, her mother, and her sisters of her plans. Bessie had moved from Walter's apartment to her own small place on Indiana Avenue on the South Side, but she saw her family often. All of them were excited by Bessie's news, but they also worried.

In the 1920s, flying was dangerous. Pilots navigated, or mapped their flying routes, mostly by guesswork. Airplanes had open cockpits and few navigation tools. Crashes were common. Pilots were popularly known as "flying fools." Bessie's family knew the dangers. They saw the difficulty and pain she faced trying to find a teacher. And they worried about Bessie leaving the country.

Even though she loved and respected her family, Bessie didn't let them discourage her. She had Robert Abbott's support. She was aiming to do something important with her life. She also discussed her plans with her husband, Claude Glenn. He went along with her wishes to learn to fly in France.

> ## IT'S A FACT!
> Bessie trained her sister Georgia to take over her manicurist job at the barbershop. But Bessie continued to do manicures for special customers.

When she needed advice, Bessie didn't turn to her family. She had come to regard Robert Abbott as her key adviser. In fact, when Robert suggested she take a better-paying job managing a chili parlor, or restaurant, she did just that.

LEARNING TO FLY

By the fall of 1920, Bessie knew where she would be learning to fly. Robert had located a school in France that was willing to teach her. On November 4, 1920, she applied for an American passport in Chicago. The passport would allow her to travel outside the United States.

On her application, Bessie gave her age as younger than it actually was. She figured being an African American woman pilot would be big news.

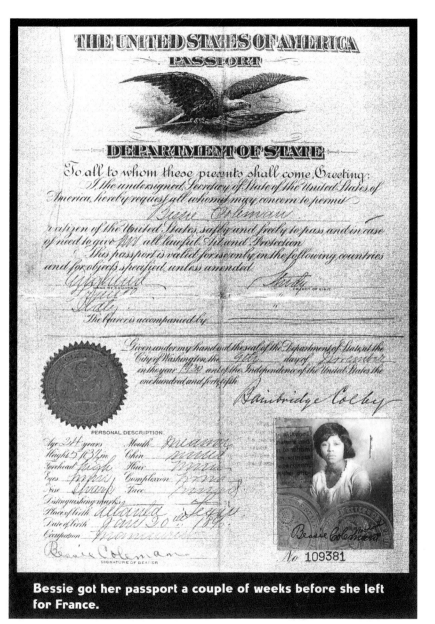

Bessie got her passport a couple of weeks before she left for France.

IT'S A FACT!

Bessie had no birth certificate. She often lied about her age. Most books about Bessie give her birth date as January 26, 1892. But she has also been listed as being born in 1893 and in 1896.

But she further figured that being a young African American woman pilot might create even bigger news.

After leaving her family, friends, and Robert Abbott, Bessie took the train to New York City. On November 20, she boarded the SS *Imparator* and sailed for France. Bessie took time to get used to the voyage. She'd never been so far from home. She'd never been on a ship before. She'd spent many years in a major U.S. city that had specific African American and white areas. Expecting something similar on the ship, she was surprised with the friendliness of the white passengers. She found this strange. It was as if leaving the shores of the United States changed their usual attitudes.

Upon arriving in France, Bessie first went to Paris, the capital city of France. She was looking for the school that Abbott had told her about. Finding the school was easy enough. But enrolling as a

Cars, carts, and people crowded Paris's streets near the famous Arc de Triomphe in the 1920s.

student was another matter. Two women students had recently died in crashes. The school's teachers decided that women weren't meant to fly. Alone and in a foreign country, Bessie was forced to look for another school. Her task wasn't made any easier by her limited ability to speak French. Despite this limitation, Bessie ended up enrolling at one of France's best aviation, or flying, schools.

In December 1920, Bessie Coleman began
taking flying lessons at the École d'Aviation des
Frères Caudron. Set up by two brothers–pilots and
plane builders René and Gaston Caudron–the
school was located at Le Crotoy. The town is in
northwestern France near the English Channel.

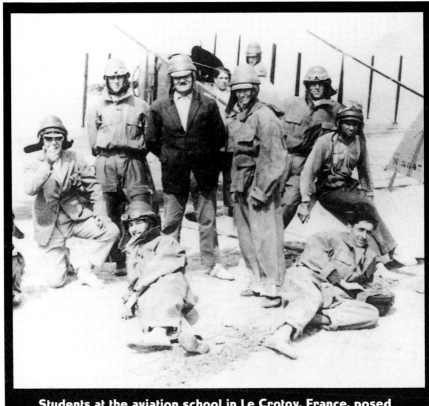

**Students at the aviation school in Le Crotoy, France, posed
during a break from flying.**

WORLD WAR I PLANES

After World War 1 ended in 1918, the planes used in the war became surplus. This meant they could be sold for nonmilitary uses. Three of the planes that became familiar to Bessie were the Nieuport 80 biplane (France), the Fokker (Germany), and the Curtiss JN-4 (United States).

The French continued to develop the Nieuport throughout the war. It was originally meant to be a racing plane, so it was light and easy to handle. It could climb higher than most other planes of the time. Anthony Fokker, a Dutch man married to a German, developed planes for the Germans. His planes were small in size but easy to handle. Germany's best pilots often flew Fokkers in dogfights, or one-on-one combat, in the sky.

The Curtiss JN-4, or Jenny, was the two-seater plane Bessie most often flew. The U.S. Army had ordered many Jennies for use in World War 1. Many American, British, and Canadian military pilots trained in Jennies. The planes were also fitted with guns for use as bombers.

A Fokker biplane

Bessie had this portrait taken while she was in France.

Bessie flew a French Nieuport 80 biplane. This type of airplane has two sets of wings stacked one on top of the other. It had become popular during World War I. Bessie remembered seeing newsreels of the Nieuport in battle. She was excited to be flying the same plane in French skies.

Bessie's lessons included everything from banked turns (veering steeply) to looping the loop (making circular turns). She also learned to take care of her aircraft. Some days, Bessie found it hard to believe she'd left Chicago to take flying lessons in France. That excitement helped her overcome feelings of loneliness. She was the only African American in Le Crotoy, and she missed her friends and family.

EARNING HER LICENSE

In spite of being lonely, Bessie worked hard. By June, she had finished her training and was ready to apply for a pilot's license. She passed her tests on the first try!

Bessie earned her pilot's license in 1921.

The Fédération Aéronautique Internationale issued Bessie's pilot's license on June 15, 1921. The small piece of paper, written in French and showing Bessie's serious face, was a great achievement. Bessie sent a letter filled with excitement to Robert Abbott. She had reason to be proud. At twenty-nine, Bessie Coleman had become the first African American woman in the world to earn a pilot's license. [N8]

IT'S A FACT!

Amelia Earhart, another U.S. female flyer, earned her license a year after Bessie Coleman. As a fairly well-to-do white woman, Earhart was able to take lessons in the United States.

Bessie's vision and determination had paid off. But she knew she had much more to learn. When her courses were over, Bessie left Le Crotoy and headed back to Paris. She hoped to take more lessons at Le Bourget Field just outside the city. Arriving in June, Bessie found the city teeming with tourists from all over Europe and America.

Over the next few months, Bessie continued her flying lessons. She also spent time learning about Paris. Unlike in the United States, Bessie could move freely through all parts of the city. The limits she'd experienced in Chicago didn't seem to exist in Paris. Instead, she felt surrounded by people who loved pilots and planes and flying. Everyone seemed to be interested in aviation. But Bessie knew that when her money ran out, she'd have to return home. When her money ran low, she made plans for her return trip.

New Insights

During World War 1, African American soldiers learned that France was color blind. This meant that French people didn't treat them differently because of their race. Even though these soldiers were mostly laborers during the war, they still experienced more freedom and earned more respect than they did in the United States.

Many soldiers stayed in France after the war. Some of them introduced parts of African American culture to France. One of these parts was jazz music. Drummers, such as Noble Sissle, and band leaders, such as James Reese—both members of the 369th Expeditionary Force—performed in France. Male and female singers found that French people liked their style. Meanwhile, as African Americans returned home, they remembered how they'd been treated by the color-blind French.

RETURNING HOME

In September 1921, Bessie left Cherbourg, France, on the SS *Manchuria*. She was on her way home. Only ten months had passed, but she was a different woman. She'd grown up and had experienced another part—a more open-minded part—of the world. With her pilot's license in hand, Bessie set her sights on New York City.

Bessie returned to New York City by boat in 1921.

The SS *Manchuria* docked at New York's harbor in late September. Bessie was surprised at the crowd of reporters—both black and white—who were there to greet her. They came from the *New York Tribune,* the *Aerial Age Weekly,* the *Air Service News,* and other newspapers. All of the reporters wanted to interview Bessie Coleman, the pilot.

As soon as Bessie left the ship, she was surrounded. Robert Abbott had been right. An African American woman pilot was big news. Front-page stories on the young flyer appeared in the *Chicago Defender* and in African American-owned newspapers across the country. White-owned newspapers reported on Coleman's accomplishments as well.

Bessie was soon in demand all over New York City. She was guest speaker at several African American churches and social clubs. Bessie was also guest of honor at a performance of the musical *Shuffle Along.* The all-African American musical had been the rage in New York City that summer. Among the *Shuffle Along* cast were Eubie Blake, Noble Sissle, Ethel Waters, and other famous performers.

Bessie's mother, Susan Coleman, poses with the silver cup given to her daughter by the cast of *Shuffle Along* in New York.

At intermission, Bessie was asked to appear onstage. Ethel Waters presented her with a silver cup engraved with the names of the cast members. The audience was segregated, with white patrons in the better seats and African American patrons in the balcony. Both groups applauded Bessie.

REACHING FOR NEW DREAMS

AS BESSIE RODE THE TRAIN back to Chicago from New York, she thought about how far she'd come in her career. She was grateful for the help of Robert Abbott. She wanted to help others— especially young African American men and women—the way Abbott had helped her. Bessie soon thought of a way. She would open her own flight school. She would give flying lessons to anyone who wanted to learn.

BIG PLANS

When the train pulled into Chicago's Union Station, Bessie looked out the window. She saw Robert

Abbott, as well as her sister Georgia. Bessie pulled her license from her purse to show them both.

Robert Abbott wanted to be sure that everyone heard the news about Bessie Coleman. First, he published a photograph of the license, with its portrait of Bessie in flying gear, in the *Defender*. The

A portrait of Bessie in her aviator's cap and goggles

following week, the newspaper featured an
interview with Bessie. In the interview, she spoke of
her desire to open a flight school for African
American men and women.

Back home on the South Side, she couldn't
stop talking about her dreams for the future. To
raise money for a school, she declared that she was
going to stage a series of exhibitions. To attract
spectators, each exhibition would have stunts (or
dangerous flying acts). Bessie's family was thrilled
with her accomplishment of getting her license. But
they were worried about the dangers of her new
career. Exhibition flying, Bessie's family knew,
could be very risky.

By the 1920s, airplanes were no longer new to
the public. If Bessie wanted to draw crowds, she
would have to perform thrilling stunts. Such stunts
were difficult. Bessie soon decided she needed
more training.

In February 1922, Bessie returned to Europe.
She trained in France for two months and then in
Germany for ten weeks. She learned to fly more
complex planes, such as the Fokker aircraft. She
met the designer of the plane, Anthony Fokker. This
additional training gave her a better sense of how to

During her second visit to Europe, Bessie (*left*) met Anthony Fokker (*right*), the airplane manufacturer.

control an airplane in flight. While in Germany, she spent time with the aviation crowd, as well as the rich and important people of German society. She was also filmed flying over the German city of Berlin. She managed to get a copy of the newsreel.

It's a Fact!

When she spoke to groups, Bessie showed the newsreel of her flights in Germany. This film was later lost.

By the first week in August, Bessie was sailing home. When the SS *Noordam* docked in New York on August 13, 1922, reporters were again there to meet her.

FIRST AIR SHOWS

With the support of the *Defender*, Bessie was the star attraction at an exhibition air show on September 3 in Long Island, New York. The excuse for having the show was to honor the Fifteenth New York Infantry. This group was part of the U.S. Army's all-African American 369th American Expeditionary Force of World War I.

Bessie wanted everyone to hear about her first American flight. By the time the Long Island air show came around, she had made waves throughout New York City. Bessie shared the bill that day with parachutist

IT'S A FACT!

Before the Long Island exhibition, Bessie talked to reporters. To build up the excitement for the show, she stretched the truth a bit. Instead of talking about chili parlors and barbershops, she told one reporter she'd learned to fly in France after going there as a Red Cross nurse.

Hubert Fauntleroy Julian, who was nicknamed the
"Black Eagle."

Men from the Fifteenth Infantry paraded
around the field. A military band played jazz tunes.
Then Bessie came out, dressed in a military-style

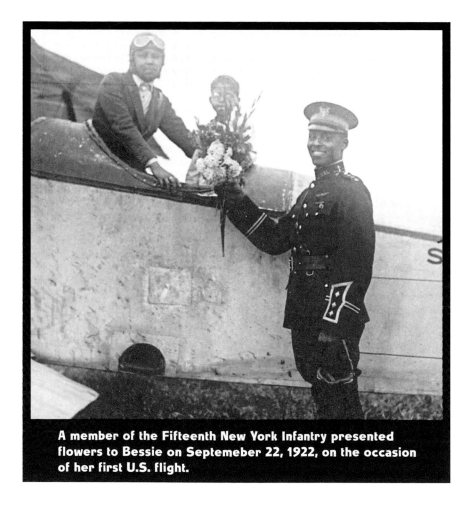

A member of the Fifteenth New York Infantry presented
flowers to Bessie on Septemeber 22, 1922, on the occasion
of her first U.S. flight.

uniform designed especially for her. Bessie flew a Curtiss JN-4, nicknamed a Jenny. The band played the "Star-Spangled Banner" as the world's only licensed African American woman pilot made her first public flight.

The Long Island exhibition was a huge success. As a result, Bessie was soon booked to perform at an African American air show in Memphis, Tennessee. Thousands of people came out to see Bessie's gutsy flying stunts. The Tennessee show was also a big success. With two successful exhibition flights behind her, Bessie Coleman was ready to return to Chicago. She felt confident enough to show the hometown folks what she could do.

She did have one problem to overcome, however. She didn't own a plane. In another example of stretching the truth, Bessie had boasted to reporters about the airplanes she'd ordered in Europe. The truth was Bessie still didn't have the money to buy a plane of her own.

Soon after Bessie's return to Chicago, a small column appeared in the *Defender*. It announced a flying exhibition to be held at Checkerboard Field in Chicago on October 15, 1922. The show would feature Chicago's own, Bessie Coleman.

Excitement swept through the South Side
community. The *Defender* offices were swamped
with messages.

Despite her outward calm, Bessie was very
nervous. She was still a new pilot. And this

**Bessie tried out
different outfits for
her flying exhibitions.
Many of the outfits
looked like military
uniforms.**

exhibition would be in front of her family, friends, and a big hometown crowd. She didn't want to let them down. Maybe her family was right. Maybe she should quit flying and be satisfied with having earned her license.

With self-doubt getting her down, Bessie went to see Robert. He did his best to calm her fears. After considerable thought, Bessie decided to go ahead. She had spent enough time in the air to know she wanted to fly for a living. Even though Bessie could earn money by managing a chili parlor, she didn't choose that safe job. She loved flying too much to consider any other way.

STUNTS IN CHICAGO

Before long, Bessie was spending hours at Checkerboard Field. She wanted to get to know the borrowed biplane she would fly. She wanted to practice her stunts so she'd be ready for the exhibition. October 15, 1922, was a glorious fall day. The Chicago airfield was packed with both black and white spectators. Among the buzzing crowd was Bessie's eight-year-old nephew from Flint, Michigan, Arthur Freeman, Nilus's boy. Most of the other Coleman family members were also there.

When she was practicing, Bessie dressed in a simple coverall rather than the uniforms she wore for exhibitions.

Young Arthur wanted to ride with his aunt Bessie. But so did a long line of other relatives and strangers. They were all hoping to fly with the famous pilot. The price was five dollars a ride. This was a lot of money at the time.

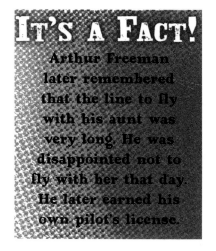

IT'S A FACT!

Arthur Freeman later remembered that the line to fly with his aunt was very long. He was disappointed not to fly with her that day. He later earned his own pilot's license.

To Arthur and to others in the crowd, Bessie seemed fearless. She sat in the open cockpit. Her neck scarf was flowing behind her in the wind. She waved to the crowd and performed all kinds of flying stunts. But the best was yet to come.

For a final act, she pulled back on the control stick, which controlled the direction of the plane. Using the control stick, she aimed the nose of her plane skyward. The engine strained to stay in operation. Even when it seemed she couldn't go any higher, Bessie continued to press the biplane up. Then the plane reached the limits of its climb. Its engine suddenly died. The crowd below fell silent. They were convinced this was the end of Bessie Coleman and her borrowed plane. Everyone craned their necks to see the crash that was sure to come.

The plane put its nose down. It dropped closer and closer to the ground. People scattered to get out of its way. At the last moment, Bessie kicked the engine back to life. Bessie hauled back hard on the stick and brought the plane out of its nosedive. When the biplane shot over their heads, people went crazy. To top off the stunt, Bessie spun the plane around in a victory roll. She touched down and drove the plane close to the gathering crowd.

LOCAL HEROINE

Even Bessie was amazed at the skills she'd shown that fall day. Her self-doubt had eased. On top of that, the air show had earned her almost one thousand dollars. Bessie opened up an account at the Binga State Bank, owned by Jesse Binga, an African American businessman. She was on her way to saving for a first payment on the flight school she wanted to open.

Chicago's African American community welcomed Bessie as a local heroine. Everywhere

Bessie enjoyed being a celebrity in Chicago.

she went, people mobbed her for her autograph. They loved her stylish scarf and her winning smile. Bessie's natural charm and good looks fit perfectly with her newfound role. For the time being anyway, she didn't have to worry about going back to work at the chili parlor or the barbershop. She was in demand as a paid speaker at African American churches and social clubs throughout Chicago.

Soon other African American-owned newspapers—like the *Pittsburgh Courier* and the

California Eagle–were covering Bessie's stunts. Her fame was spreading. Her mail was full of invitations to speak in other parts of the country.

Bessie discussed her next move with Robert Abbott. Meanwhile, Georgia and the rest of the family were being won over to Bessie's side. They were both scared and proud of her first appearance at Checkerboard Field. They realized that Bessie had found something she truly loved. Chances to earn money flying in Chicago were limited, however. To raise money to open her own school, Bessie would have to perform in more exhibitions in other parts of the country.

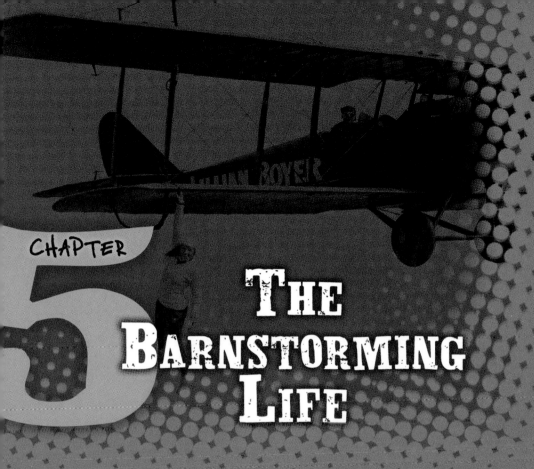

CHAPTER 5

THE BARNSTORMING LIFE

WHILE STUDYING IN FRANCE,
Bessie realized that just having a license to
fly wouldn't guarantee a job as a pilot. At
that time, commercial airlines (taking
paying passengers from city to city) were
still in the future. The U.S. airmail service
hired pilots, but only white men.

In the 1920s, however, most pilots
traveled from place to place looking for

(Above)
Air shows
were full of
dangerous
stunts. Here
a flyer hangs
from the
wing of a
plane in
flight in 1923.

69

work. They charged a fee to take up brave customers in the air for a ride. Otherwise, these traveling pilots would try to find work at county fairs by adding some flying thrills. They'd also comb the countryside looking for passengers who needed to get someplace quickly and for deliveries between towns. Often, when fuel ran low or when the sun went down and they could no longer navigate, they would be forced to land in fields or in farmlands. They might even find themselves sleeping in barns at night. People called these pilots barnstormers, because they stormed the countryside, looking for ways to earn a living. It wasn't a safe life, but these pilots were risk takers and adventurers. In 1923, when thirty-one-year-old Bessie took up the barnstorming life, she was no different.

TRYING OUT CALIFORNIA

After the publicity died down from the Checkerboard Field exhibition, Bessie set her sights on California. She thought Los Angeles would be a great place to pursue her dream. The growing city in southwestern California was becoming the center of the nation's new flying and movie industries. Soon Bessie was discussing plans for a trip west.

Bessie left wintry Chicago in late January 1923. She headed first to Oakland, a city in northern California near San Francisco. She was setting up a deal with the Coast Tire and Rubber Company, which was located in that city. Under the deal, Bessie would represent Coast Tire at public events. She would also put the company's logo on the planes she flew. Several white pilots had similar deals, but Bessie was the first African American flyer to make such an agreement with a major corporation.

After completing this arrangement with Coast Tire, she headed south for Los Angeles. The African American population in Los Angeles was centered along Central Avenue. Between 1910 and 1920, factory jobs had drawn many African Americans to the city. The workers made airplanes and military equipment at the city's factories. By the time Bessie arrived, the Central Avenue community was doing well. African American businesses were everywhere. The community had African American meeting places and hotels. An African American hospital was in place. And five African American newspapers

IT'S A FACT!

Bessie's reputation arrived in Los Angeles before she did. The *California Eagle*, the best known of the area's African American newspapers, had covered her adventures during the past year.

provided news. Several social clubs and African American churches were also in operation. Los Angeles attracted many of the best-educated and most prominent African Americans in the United States. Bessie was among the most well known.

In Los Angeles, Bessie purchased an airplane. For four hundred dollars, she was able to get a used Curtiss JN-4. Most of the money came from the first payment on her Coast Tire deal. Many Jennies had been produced as training planes during the war. After the war, pilots could buy the leftover airplanes. The planes had become quite popular with pilots, mainly because they were cheap.

Many of the flyers in the Los Angeles area flew Jennies. This put Bessie at ease because she knew the plane well. She also liked Los Angeles, with its growing businesses scattered along Central Avenue. Bessie decided that her move westward

A Central Avenue pharmacist stands outside his shop. In this black community of Los Angeles, many African Americans owned their own businesses.

was the right choice. Perhaps the city was even the right place to start her aviation school.

FIRST CRASH

Bessie made a point of visiting with all the local African American newspapers to tell them of her plans. Likely to exaggerate, Bessie painted a very ambitious picture of an aviation school for

African Americans, complete with a fleet of top-notch airplanes.

The truth could hardly be more different. Once Bessie's lone plane—the recently purchased Jenny—was ready, she attempted to set up an exhibition flight at Rogers Field in Los Angeles. But

IT'S A FACT!

Amelia Earhart took her first plane ride at Rogers Field in Los Angeles in 1920.

when her financial backers pulled out at the last moment, Bessie's plans fell through. Coast Tire had helped her buy the Jenny, but the company refused Bessie more support.

Bessie spent the next few weeks scrambling for new backers. Finally, she succeeded in finding enough support to schedule another exhibition. Set for February 4, 1923, this exhibition would take place at Palomar Park in Los Angeles. Bessie was sure she would draw a good crowd since she had gotten good publicity after arriving in Los Angeles.

This time, everything seemed to be working out just right. Bessie was to be the sole attraction at Palomar Park. Long before Bessie was due to fly, nearly ten thousand people had gathered at the park.

Bessie with her first airplane, a Curtiss JN-4. The airplane was made mainly of wires, wood, and canvas.

Bessie's excitement was matched by that of the large and mostly African American crowd.

When Bessie took off from nearby Santa Monica, where her plane had been parked, she felt confident. The plane had recently been checked out, and the park was only a short hop away. While the biplane rose above the city streets, Bessie went over her plans for the air show. She would try another gutsy landing, just as she had at Checkerboard Field, along with other stunts.

To raise money for exhibitions, Bessie wrote many letters. Her writing paper showed her portrait and a sample of her more daring stunts.

JENNY JINX?

The Curtiss JN-4 had long been used as a flight training airplane. Flight instructors felt that a trainee who could pilot a Jenny was likely able to pilot anything. The Jenny could be a bit sluggish and had a very poor climbing rate. The engine often stalled while in the air, and pilots could find it tricky to get the engine to kick in again. About 20 percent of all Jennies crashed during flight training.

But soon after takeoff, Bessie's planning ended. The Jenny's motor stalled, and the biplane began a quick fall, nose down to the streets below. Bessie tried to pull out of the dive but failed. The Jenny hit the ground, and its pilot lay motionless.

Bessie was lucky the Jenny was flying at only three hundred feet when the motor stalled. When she was pulled out of the wreckage, she was unconscious but still alive. A doctor at the site of the crash did what he could, but Bessie had to be transported to Saint Catherine's Hospital in Santa Monica. After she came to, Bessie discovered that she had broken one leg and fractured several ribs. Her face showed cuts and bruises, and she had injuries inside her body as well. This was her first crash. She hoped she would never have another.

TIME TO HEAL

Bessie would have plenty of time to think about the dangers of her chosen career while she was being patched up and cared for at the hospital. She was in pain from her injuries, from losing her only airplane and, perhaps worst of all, from letting down the thousands of spectators who had awaited her arrival at Palomar Park in Los Angeles.

As Bessie was rushed to the hospital, spectators at Palomar Park had grown angry. Many had demanded a refund of their money. Bessie could hardly blame them. She hated disappointing her fans.

IT'S A FACT!
Bessie eventually sent a telegram to her fans, telling them that as soon as she could walk, she'd get back to flying.

Meanwhile, word of Bessie's crash reached Chicago. Susan Coleman, Elois, Georgia, and the others were all concerned and worried. Bessie soon sent word to her family and friends that she was going to be fine. But she was not free from worry.

Her broken leg was taking far longer to heal than she had planned. As she got better in the hospital over the next few weeks, Bessie continued to plot and plan. The crash had been a setback, no doubt about it. But nothing was going to stop her from opening a flying school.

In May 1923, Bessie finally hobbled out of the hospital on crutches. For the rest of that month, she stayed at a friend's home in Los Angeles. She gave a few lectures and showed films of her earlier flights. By June, however, Bessie was ready to head back to Chicago. She was without a plane. Her pockets were empty. Her nearly six-month stay in sunny California had not been a financial success.

6 BACK TO TEXAS

BEING BROKE DID NOT discourage Bessie for long. Once back in Chicago, she arranged to be part of an air show in Columbus, Ohio, on Labor Day, that September. Rain poured down on the day, and Bessie's heart sank. Another show had been canceled. Another crowd had been let down. Bessie went back to Chicago until the following weekend. She hoped her luck might change at the rescheduled air show.

BACK IN THE AIR

An upbeat crowd was at the fairgrounds for the rescheduled show. Bessie was pretty good at estimating crowds by now. She was sure at least ten thousand people were there, enjoying the sunshine. All in all, Bessie couldn't have hoped for a better day. Her borrowed plane responded easily. And her spirits received the lift they so desperately needed. Her show was a great success. Her fans started calling her Queen Bess.

Back in Chicago after this triumph, Bessie was full of plans. Soon, she told a reporter from the *Chicago Defender,* she was going to give a farewell flight to her hometown. Then she would barnstorm the South.

But although her fans waited expectantly, nothing happened. No farewell flight or southern tour ever happened, and Bessie's boasting cost her some fans and friends. To make matters worse, her string of bad luck had cooled the interest of her first supporter, Robert Abbott. He let her know he was no longer interested in promoting her many plans and adventures. She had disappointed him by setting up expectations she couldn't meet.

Bessie settled into an apartment on South Parkway to rest and think about her future. Despite her achievements, she found that she didn't fit into Chicago's African American middle-class society. To many African American Chicagoans, such as Robert Abbott, Bessie Coleman seemed too hard to figure out.

Bessie's family, however, was happy to have her home again. Her apartment became the gathering place for sisters, brothers, nieces, and nephews. Bessie was a world traveler, a famous flyer, and a hero. She had done more than any other Coleman had ever done! Her nieces and nephews loved to hear her stories.

In Houston

This routine life suited Bessie fine for a while. Then in early 1925, she felt she had to move on. Her dreams had not died, despite the setbacks.

Thirty-three years after her birth, Bessie decided to gear up and head back to Texas. In the years since she had left her home state, Bessie had amounted to something. The former cotton picker and maid was now the only licensed African American woman pilot in the whole world. She was fluent in French. She was a world traveler. She was polished. Yet she was returning to Texas to launch a comeback. Bessie

Coleman was trying to escape the bad luck that
seemed to follow her. The city of Houston, Texas,
would be her new base of operations.

On May 9, 1925, Bessie gave her first lecture
in Houston. Along with a
short speech, she showed
films of her flights. Her
experiences were unique,
and the Houston audience
seemed to like her. Over
the next few weeks,
Bessie gave several
lectures. All the
audiences were eager to
meet her.

IT'S A FACT!
Bessie's Houston
lecture helped her
raise money. This
wasn't just to cover
her expenses. She
still dreamed of
owning her own
brand-new plane.

Five weeks after she arrived in Houston,
Bessie took her first flight. She had to borrow a
plane, but she was determined to get off the
ground. The air show was set for June 19, or
Juneteenth, an African American holiday. Again,
Bessie's reputation preceded her. The stands were
full of white spectators—while the African
American audience stood on a dirt surface.
Everyone there was very interested in seeing the
famous Bessie Coleman fly an airplane.

JUNETEENTH

Celebrated on June 19, Juneteenth is the country's oldest known holiday honoring the end of slavery. This was the date in 1865 when African American slaves in Texas learned that they were free.

Texas was far away from much of the fighting of the Civil War (1861–1865). But in 1865, Union troops of the North landed at Galveston, Texas. Texas, a southern state, had been fighting on the side of the Confederacy, or the South. In April 1865, the South surrendered to the North. The Civil War was over.

More than two years before, however, in January 1863, President Abraham Lincoln had sent out an important message, or proclamation. It was called the Emancipation Proclamation. As of January 1, 1863, the proclamation said all slaves under the Confederacy would be free (emancipated). But why did it take so long for the information to reach Texas?

Lots of people have tried to explain the delay. One story goes that the messenger with the news was murdered on the way to Texas. Another was that slave owners kept back the news to keep their unpaid workforce of slaves. Still another says the Union troops stalled to allow the slave owners to finish one last harvest of cotton. No one knows for sure what the truth is.

But starting in 1865, African Americans in Texas informally celebrated the date. It became a time to share good food, to hear stories of bravery, and to be with family. In 1980, Texas made the holiday official. Other cities around the country—including Milwaukee, Wisconsin, and Minneapolis, Minnesota—followed. Modern Juneteenth celebrations honor African American culture, without forgetting the historic roots of the holiday in Texas.

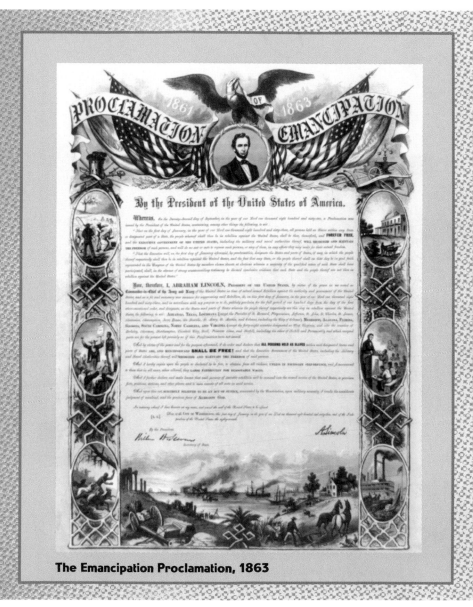

The Emancipation Proclamation, 1863

Publicity photos, like this undated portrait of Bessie with a Jenny, were likely to be printed in black-owned newspapers in areas where Bessie made her flights.

Bessie performed magnificently, just as she had done in her Chicago exhibition at Checkerboard Field and later in Columbus. She performed many of her usual stunts, adding barrel rolls and figure eights. (In a barrel roll, the plane spins over by its width. The route followed in a figure eight looks like the number eight.) Her accident in California didn't seem to have made her any less daring.

NEW TRAVELS

Thousands of fans had a glorious Juneteenth in Houston that year, thanks to Bessie Coleman. Many of her bravest fans paid for the chance to ride in the plane with Queen Bess herself.

At that time in Texas, it was still unusual to see an airplane, much less an airplane piloted by an African American woman. So many people were curious to see her that Bessie hoped to make a fairly good living there.

Over the next few weeks, she made appearances in Houston, San Antonio, Dallas, Fort Worth, and smaller Texas towns in between—including Waxahachie, Bessie's old hometown. At each of these stops, Bessie was either lecturing or flying. Early in the fall of 1925, Bessie returned home to Chicago for a break. She wanted to see her family and rest for a bit. She had money in the bank. Her mind and body were fully healed. She was healthy, high-spirited, and feeling confident once again.

After a three-month stay, Bessie was ready to go back on the road—a life she had grown to love. She would soon be lecturing again, this time in Georgia and Florida. Bessie spent Christmas Eve 1925 with Elois, wrapping gifts and talking through the night. Then she left for Savannah, Georgia.

Her first lecture was at a local theater. The African American weekly *Savannah Tribune* told of the community's excitement at hosting this famous visitor. Bessie gave lectures in Augusta and Atlanta as well. She then headed for Florida, where she spoke and showed films of her flights in Saint Petersburg, Tampa, and West Palm Beach. At this rate, with the profits from her Texas tour and a successful Florida trip, she would soon be close to her goal. By the spring of 1927, she might even have enough money to open her own school.

CHAPTER 7
FLYING HIGH IN FLORIDA

BESSIE'S LECTURES were very popular. People especially liked watching films of her flights. She was drawing crowds at all her stops. In 1926, Bessie was seriously thinking about having a movie made about her flights and career. After all, the movie industry, like the aviation industry, was still young.

(Above) **Bessie (*right*) poses with a friend.**

Bessie's letter to Norman Studios

In February 1926, Bessie wrote a letter to a
movie producer at Norman Studios in Florida.
Bessie expressed her desire to put her life on film.
She was convinced a movie of her life would be a
big hit. After all, her story was unique, full of
adventure, and sure to draw her many fans.

TRYING AGAIN

When nothing came of Bessie's movie idea with
Norman Studios, she didn't get too discouraged.
Instead, she continued lecturing but kept her

focus on raising money for her flying school. She worked part-time in a beauty parlor in Orlando, Florida, and flew as often as she could. But getting up in the air was a constant struggle.

Bessie didn't own a plane while in Florida. In fact, she hadn't owned one since she had crashed her Jenny in California. Whenever she flew in Chicago, Florida, or Texas, Bessie had had to borrow a plane. This limited her ability to fly in air shows and to take people up for rides. It also limited her ability to earn money. Still, Bessie did manage to give an exhibition using a borrowed airplane in West Palm Beach early in 1926.

Some months before, Bessie had made a down payment on a plane of her own in Dallas. Try as she might, Bessie couldn't find the money to pay it

IT'S A FACT!

In addition to movies made in Hollywood, African American and white filmmakers were also producing race movies. These movies were meant for African American audiences. They were often shown at midnight, when whites were not using the theater. Or they were shown in movie theaters owned by African Americans.

IT'S A FACT!

Often Bessie was able to borrow a plane from local white pilots. For some reason, white pilots seemed less racist than other whites. Perhaps because they shared a special bond—the love of flying—these flyers felt a kinship not found in the rest of American society.

off. So while an old Curtiss Jenny sat waiting for her in Dallas, Bessie scrambled to discover some way to raise more funds so she could get her plane to Florida.

In February 1926, Bessie met Edwin M. Beeman, heir to the Beeman chewing gum fortune. When Beeman gave her money to make the final payment on her plane in Dallas, the young pilot thought her troubles were over. With Beeman's support, Bessie made arrangements to have her plane flown to Jacksonville, Florida. The Jacksonville Negro Welfare League had invited her to perform there on May 1, and she planned to use her new plane.

BESSIE AND WILLIAM WILLS

Jacksonville, like most Florida cities, was completely segregated. African Americans and

The Jacksonville, Florida, train station had separate waiting rooms for African American and white passengers.

whites lived and worked separately. All the same, the white newspaper in Jacksonville ran a story announcing Bessie's upcoming exhibition. Bessie was also making headlines in the African American community. She was booked for a number of speaking engagements in churches and theaters and at local all-African American public schools. Increasingly, Bessie was taking her message to African American children. They seemed more eager to learn about flying than adults—and more likely to enroll in her school.

While Bessie was on her way to Jacksonville, a young white mechanic named William D. Wills was leaving Love Field in Dallas. Wills had agreed to pilot the Jenny, an even older version than the first Jenny she had owned in California. This was the type of airplane she had to settle for. Without more money coming in on a regular basis, Bessie could never afford anything better, newer, or safer.

William D. Wills flew an old Jenny from Dallas, Texas, to Jacksonville, Florida, so Bessie could buy it.

Even during the short flight from Dallas to Jacksonville, the plane had problems. Wills had to land in Meridian and Farmingdale in Mississippi. At each stop, he made repairs to the struggling Jenny. Despite these problems, Wills landed in Jacksonville, Florida, on April 28. Local pilots who met Wills were surprised that he managed to pilot the old plane so far.

On April 30, Bessie met Wills at Paxon Field in Jacksonville to try out the Jenny. She was looking forward to flying her own plane at last. Bessie and Wills planned to fly over a nearby racetrack, the site of the next day's exhibition for the Negro Welfare League.

THE FATAL FLIGHT

For one of her planned stunts, Bessie would be trying something different. She would make a parachute jump from the wings of the Jenny. So for their trial run, William Wills took the controls, while Bessie sat behind him. The Jenny rose high above Jacksonville, climbing to two thousand and then to thirty-five hundred feet. Bessie didn't wear her seatbelt. She wanted to lean over the side to see the field. Wills circled so Bessie could view the racetrack and then turned back.

Suddenly the plane raced forward, and the Jenny began a quick, spinning dive toward the ground. William Wills tried to regain control of the spinning Jenny. He failed. As the plane spun downward, Bessie was thrown from her seat. She fell to her death. William Wills stayed at the controls until the Jenny crashed onto farmland. Not far away lay Bessie Coleman's crushed body. Wills died soon afterward. Coleman's body was taken to a local African American-owned funeral home. Wills's body was taken to a white-owned funeral home.

Meanwhile, officials searched for and found the cause of the accident. A wrench had slid into the control gears. The wrench had gotten tangled up with the gears. The gears had jammed, making the plane impossible to control. Local aviators said that the accident would not have happened if Bessie had been piloting a newer plane. On new planes, the gears were covered. A wrench wouldn't have been able to touch them.

However, Bessie had no choice. She wanted to fly. As with many other things in a segregated

William Wills died in the wreckage of the plane crash. Bessie's body was found one thousand feet away.

society, an African American often has to make do with second best, sometimes with deadly results. Bessie had faced this fact her whole life, but she didn't let it hold her back. To her death, she had resisted society's boundaries for African Americans and for women.

HONORING BESSIE

A memorial service was held in Jacksonville, Florida. Nearly five thousand people mourned Bessie. A memorial service was also held in Orlando, Florida. Then Bessie's body was sent by train to Chicago to be with her family.

For the funeral service at Chicago's Pilgrim Baptist Church in May of 1926, nearly fifteen hundred family, friends, and fans crowded the pews. Outside, thousands more milled about, unable to get in. Among the pallbearers, speakers, and mourners at Bessie Coleman's final memorial were the finest of Chicago's African American community. Bessie had arrived by train from Texas in 1915 as an unknown cotton picker. She was honored eleven years later as a shining light the world over.

Bessie Coleman and other early pilots were on the cutting edge of a new industry. But unlike other pilots, Bessie had to overcome the obstacle of being a woman and an African American. From humble beginnings in Texas to her death as a celebrated aviator in Florida, she followed her dream and paved the way for others. She realized that part of her mission was to encourage other African

Bessie Coleman, 1892–1926

Americans to get into aviation. Bessie Coleman
remained an inspiration for African American men
and women for many years to come.

THE BESSIE COLEMAN AERO CLUB

Among the people at Bessie's memorial was a successful business owner named William J. Powell. He owned several service stations and a garage in Chicago. Like Bessie Coleman, he had been bitten by the aviation bug.

William J. Powell was inspired by the life and achievements of Bessie Coleman.

Powell had followed Bessie's career closely. He had read everything he could about her, whether in the *Defender,* the *California Eagle,* the *Pittsburgh Courier,* or other newspapers. Soon after Coleman's burial in 1926, Powell decided to sell his Chicago businesses and move to Los Angeles. He wanted to be where the flying action was. Once he had learned to fly, Powell decided to carry on Bessie's dream of opening an aviation school for African Americans. Using his skill as a businessman, Powell and others opened up the Bessie Coleman Aero Club in Los Angeles in 1929.

James Herman Banning from Ames, Iowa, was the school's main teacher. At that time, he was the country's most-experienced African American pilot. He had earned his license in 1926 from the U.S. Department of Commerce, becoming the first African American to do so.

Among Banning's students was Marie Dickerson, a noted dancer and singer performing in California. Looking through the *California Eagle* one day, Dickerson came across an advertisement for the Bessie Coleman Aero Club. She couldn't believe her eyes. Not only was there a school for African Americans, but it was named after an African American woman. When she came to Los Angeles, Marie approached the school's storefront office with a sense of pride.

Through her lessons at the Bessie Coleman Aero Club, Marie soon earned her license. She became a member of the Five Blackbirds, a flying troupe that performed at air shows. The Five Blackbirds performed at the very first all-African American air show in October 1931 at the Eastside Airport in Los Angeles. The Bessie Coleman Aero Club sponsored that historic event.

Perhaps the most important milestone of the Bessie Coleman Aero Club occurred in 1932. Banning and twenty-five-year-old ace mechanic Thomas C. Allen completed the first transcontinental flight by African American pilots. Banning and Allen left Los Angeles in a secondhand biplane on September 18 and landed in New York on October 9, 1932. Nicknamed the Flying Hobos, the two landed in New York, not as hobos but as heroes.

Bessie Coleman wasn't perfect. She made mistakes. She disappointed people. And she never saw her dream of starting a flying school come true. However, her impact is still being felt today. The

A group of African-American pilots prepare the annual dropping of flowers on Bessie Coleman's grave in Chicago.

IT'S A FACT!

In 1995, the U.S. Postal Service created a stamp honoring Bessie Coleman for her role in African American history.

BLACK HERITAGE

USA
32

BESSIE COLEMAN

individuals Bessie Coleman inspired have helped make her dream a reality. In the twenty-first century, African Americans are achieving great things in aviation as pilots, mechanics, and astronauts; in business; and in many other fields. Bessie Coleman's story tells us all that no matter how humble our beginnings, if we dare to dream, we can succeed.

1892 Bessie Coleman is born on January 26.

1894 The Coleman family moves to Waxahachie, Texas.

1901 George Coleman leaves Texas for Indian Territory (in present-day Oklahoma).

1903 Wilbur and Orville Wright's plane flies at Kitty Hawk, North Carolina.

1905 Robert Abbott publishes the first issue of the *Chicago Defender*.

1907 Indian Territory and Oklahoma Territory form the state of Oklahoma.

1910 Bessie goes to Langston College.

1911 Harriet Quimby is the first American woman to get a pilot's license.

1911 Bessie leaves Langston and returns to Texas.

1912 Quimby is killed when her airplane crashes at an air show in Boston, Massachusetts.

1914 World War I starts in Europe.

1915 Bessie moves to Chicago, Illinois.

1917 The United States enters World War I. Eugene Bullard becomes the first African American pilot.

1918 Bessie marries Claude Glenn. World War I ends.

1920 Bessie leaves the United States to take flying lessons in France.

1921 In June, Bessie earns her pilot's license, becoming the first African American woman to do so. She returns to the United States in September.

1922 Bessie returns to Europe to take more flying lessons. Bessie takes part in her first exhibition air show in New York. She performs amazing air stunts at an air show in Chicago.

1923 Bessie becomes a barnstorming pilot. She moves to California. She crashes at an air show near Los Angeles. She moves back to Chicago.

1925 Bessie starts a barnstorming tour of Texas.

1926 Bessie starts a barnstorming tour in Florida. She and her mechanic, William Wills, die when her plane crashes the day before an air show. She is buried in Chicago.

1926 James Banning earns his pilot's license becoming the first African-American aviator licensed in the United States.

1927 Charles Lindbergh completes the first solo flight across the Atlantic Ocean from New York City to Paris in *The Spirit of St. Louis.*

1929 William Powell opens the Bessie Coleman Aero Club in Los Angeles. Banning is the club's main teacher.

1931 The Bessie Coleman Aero Club sponsors the first all-African American air show in American history in Los Angeles.

1932 Banning and his mechanic are the first African Americans to fly from coast to coast.

1982 The "Black Wings: The American Black in Aviation" opens at the Smithsonian Institution's National Air and Space Museum in Washington, D.C. Bessie Coleman is included in the pioneers section of the exhibit.

1995 The U.S. Postal Service creates a stamp in honor of Bessie Coleman.

biplane: an airplane with two sets of wings

Croix de Guerre: meaning "war cross" in French, a French military award given for bravery

Distinguished Service Crosses: U.S. military awards given to those who performed especially heroic service during wartime

Fédération Aéronautique Internationale: a nongovernmental organization that oversees world air sports. Founded in 1905, its goal is to expand flying activities worldwide.

Foreign Legion: founded in 1831, a volunteer fighting unit of the French government

French Resistance: the nonmilitary group that fought the Germans just before and long after Germany occupied France during World War II

racial discrimination: an opinion formed unfairly about a racial group. Racial discrimination can lead to racial segregation, or the practice of keeping racial groups apart.

the South: in the United States, the states that fought against the Union (the North) in the Civil War (1861–1865). Bessie's home state of Texas is part of the South.

stunt: an unusual act that is usually daring or requires great skill. At air shows, pilots perform such stunts as barrel rolls, figure eights, and loop the loops to thrill the crowd.

World War I: a global conflict fought between Germany and its allies and France and its allies from 1914 to 1918 in Europe and the Middle East

World War II: a global conflict fought between Germany and Japan and their allies against the United States, France, the Soviet Union., and Britain and their allies from 1939 to 1945 in Europe, the Middle East, and Asia

SELECTED BIBLIOGRAPHY

Books:

Bragg, Janet, and Marjorie M. Kriz. *Soaring above Setbacks: The Autobiography of Janet Harmon Bragg.* With a foreword by Johnetta B. Cole. Washington DC: Smithsonian Institution Press, 1996.

Briggs, Carole S. *At the Controls: Women in Aviation.* Minneapolis: Lerner Publications Company, 1991.

Hardesty, Von, and Dominick Pisano. *Black Wings: The American Black in Aviation.* Washington, DC: National Air and Space Museum, Smithsonian Institution Press, 1983.

Hart, Philip S. *Flying Free: America's First Black Aviators.* Minneapolis: Lerner Publications Company, 1992.

Haskins, Jim. *Black Eagles: African Americans in Aviation.* New York: Scholastic, Inc., 1995.

Lynn, Jack. *The Hallelujah Flight.* New York: St. Martin's Press, 1990.

Powell, William. *Black Wings.* 1934. Rpt. as *Black Aviator: William J. Powell.* Washington, DC: Smithsonian Institution Press, 1994.

Rich, Doris L. *Queen Bess: Daredevil Aviator*. Washington, DC: Smithsonian Institution Press, 1993.

Films:

Flyers in Search of a Dream. Produced by Philip Hart in association with WGBH-Boston and UCLA. PBS documentary film. 1987.

Interviews by author:

Coker, Marie Dickerson. Student at Bessie Coleman Aero Club. Los Angeles, California, September 1983.

Freeman, Arthur. Nephew of Bessie Coleman. Los Angeles, California, September 1983.

FURTHER READING AND WEBSITES

Bessie Coleman Website
http://www.bessiecoleman.com
This website traces Bessie's roots from Texas to the end of her barnstorming life.

Black Wings
http://www.nasm.si.edu/interact/blackwings/hstory/index.html
The National Air and Space Museum shares its exhibit on African American aviators.

Borden, Louise, and Mary Kay Kroeger. *Fly High! The Story of Bessie Coleman*. New York: Margaret K. McElderry Books, 2001.

Briggs, Carole S. *Women Space Pioneers*. Minneapolis: Lerner Publications Company, 2005.

Dartford, Mark. *Fighter Planes*. Minneapolis: Lerner Publications Company, 2004.

Feldman, Ruth Tenzer. *World War I*. Minneapolis: Lerner Publications Company, 2004.

Freydberg, Elizabeth Amelia Hadley. *Bessie Coleman: The Brownskin Lady Bird*. New York: Garland Publishing, Inc. 1994.

Grimes, Nikki. *Talkin' about Bessie: The Story of Aviator Elizabeth Coleman*. New York: Scholastic, 1998.

Gubert, Betty Kaplan. *Invisible Wings: An Annotated Bibliography on Blacks in Aviation*. Westport, CT: Greenwood Press, 1994.

Hart, Philip S. *Flying Free: America's First Black Aviators*. Minneapolis: Lerner Publications Company, 1992.

Hoban, Sarah. *Daily Life in Ancient and Modern Paris*. Minneapolis: Runestone Press, 1999.

Johnson, Dolores. *She Dared to Fly: Bessie Coleman*. New York: Benchmark Books, 1997.

Lindbergh, Reeve. *Nobody Owns the Sky*. Boston: Walker Books, 1996.

Maynard, Chris. *Aircraft*. Minneapolis: LernerSports, 1999.

McPherson, Stephanie Sammartino, and Joseph Sammartino Gardner. *Wilbur & Orville Wright: Taking Flight*. Minneapolis: Carolrhoda Books, Inc., 2004.

Plantz, Connie. *Bessie Coleman: First Black Woman Pilot*. Berkeley Heights, NJ: Enslow Publishers, 2001.

Tessendorf, K.C. *Barnstormers and Daredevils*. New York: Antheum, 1988.

Women in Aviation Resource Center
http://women-in-aviation.com
This site offers information on women pilots and the different aircraft they've flown.

PHOTO ACKNOWLEDGMENTS

Images in this book are used with permission of: Library of Congress, p. 5; Library of Congress, pp. 19 (LC-USZ62-5070), 27 (LC-USZ62-17971), 85 (LC-USZ62-91360); Ellis County (TX) Museum, Inc., p. 6; © Underwood & Underwood/ CORBIS, pp. 9, 60; National Archives, p. 11 (16-G-116-1-CI19092); USDA, p. 12; Currie Ballard, Historian, Langston University, p. 15; © Smithsonian Institution, National Air and Space Museum, pp. 21 (93-16052), 30 (91-3993), 43 (93-16050), 46 (94-13746), 48 (88-7993), 49 (93-7758), 56 (80-12873), 62 (99-16415), 64, 89 (79-12284), 102 (92-15382); Chicago Historical Society, pp. 22 (ICHi-06962), 24 (ICHi-20428); © Hulton Archive/Getty Images, p. 25; Imperial War Museum, London, p. 32; © Topical Press Agency/Getty Images, p. 35; The Chicago Defender, p. 38; © Museum of Flight/CORBIS, p. 40; © PoodlesRock/CORBIS, p. 45; Denver Public Library, Western History Collection p. 47 (X-21946); © Bettmann/CORBIS, p. 52; Security Pacific National Bank Photograph Collection/Los Angeles Public Library, pp. 54, 75, 99; Courtesy Lilly Library, Indiana University, Bloomington, Indiana, pp. 58, 67, 76, 86, 90; Minnesota Historical Society, p. 69; Shades of L.A. Collection/Los Angeles Public Library, p. 73; Florida State Archives, pp. 93, 94, 97; Hatfield Collection/Museum of Flight, Seattle, p. 100; U.S. Postal Service, p. 103.

Cover image: © Underwood & Underwood/CORBIS.